I ♥ BARACK

INSPIRING WORDS FROM THE 44TH PRESIDENT

STERLING
New York

STERLING
New York

An Imprint of Sterling Publishing Co., Inc.
1166 Avenue of the Americas
New York, NY 10036

ISBN 978-1-4549-3885-9

Distributed in Canada by Sterling Publishing Co., Inc.
^{C}/o Canadian Manda Group, 664 Annette Street
Toronto, Ontario M6S 2C8, Canada
Distributed in the United Kingdom by GMC Distribution Services
Castle Place, 166 High Street, Lewes, East Sussex BN7 1XU, England
Distributed in Australia by NewSouth Books
University of New South Wales, Sydney, NSW 2052, Australia

For information about custom editions, special sales,
and premium and corporate purchases, please contact Sterling Special Sales
at 800-805-5489 or specialsales@sterlingpublishing.com

Manufactured in Canada

2 4 6 8 10 9 7 5 3 1

sterlingpublishing.com

Cover and interior book design by Scott Russo

Cover illustration by Sourav Aich

Image credits on page 368

Introduction

America under Barack Obama embraced online culture like never before, and so it's no surprise that the memetic reach of his words and actions has been so widespread. Whether singing Al Green, dancing with Ellen, or even wearing the occasional tan suit, Obama became an icon that has lived on long after his presidency.

Barack Obama's legacy embodies progress, citizens' duty to each other, and above all, hope. When the younger generations had thrown their hands up in frustration with politics, Obama made it feel personal, possible.

What follows here is a selection of the very best of our 44th president. Read in one sitting, flip through at your leisure, or keep it handy for the times when you need a pick-me-up to remind you that change doesn't happen all at once, but it does happen.

Our stories are singular, but our destiny is shared.

—Victory speech,
November 5, 2008

I'm comfortable in my own skin.

—*Rolling Stone*,
December 30, 2004

I want to especially thank all the members who took a break from their exhausting schedule of not passing any laws to be here tonight.

—White House Correspondents' Dinner,
April 29, 2012

I look so old, John Boehner's already invited Netanyahu to speak at my funeral.

—White House Correspondents' Dinner,
April 25, 2015

These days,
I look in the mirror
and I have to
admit, I'm not the
strapping young
Muslim socialist
that I used to be.

—White House Correspondents' Dinner,
April 28, 2013

One of the things I think I can bring to the presidency is to make government and public service cool again.

—Interview, *Time*, 2007

Democracy works, but we've got to want it— not just during an election year, but all the days in between.

—Democratic National Convention, July 27, 2016

We need a President who sees government not as a tool to enrich well-connected friends and high-priced lobbyists, but as the defender of fairness and opportunity for every American.

—Speech on government reform, June 22, 2007

When I was a kid, I inhaled. Frequently. That was the point.

—Speech at the American Society of Magazine Editors, October 2006

And then there's Ted Cruz. Ted had a tough week. He went to Indiana—Hoosier country—stood on a basketball court, and called the hoop a "basketball ring." What else is in his lexicon? Baseball sticks? Football hats? But sure, *I'm* the foreign one.

—White House Correspondents' Dinner, April 30, 2016

I have enjoyed working with all of you. That does not, of course, mean that I've enjoyed every story that you have filed. But that's the point of this relationship. . . . you're supposed to cast a critical eye on folks who hold enormous power and make sure that we are accountable to the people who sent us here.

—Final press conference, January 18, 2017

My job is not to represent Washington to you, but to represent you to Washington.

—*Oprah Winfrey Show*, October 18, 2006

Change is never easy, but always possible.

—NAACP Fight for Freedom Fund Dinner,
May 1, 2005

I love the press.
I even sat for an
interview with Bill
O'Reilly right before
the Super Bowl.
That was a change
of pace. I don't often
get a chance to be in
a room with an ego
that's bigger than mine.

—Gridiron Club Dinner,
March 12, 2011

I spent a lot of time in my farewell address talking about the state of our democracy. It goes without saying that essential to that is a free press. That is part of how this place, this country, this grand experiment in self-government has to work. It doesn't work if we don't have a well-informed citizenry.

—Final press conference, January 18, 2017

We were strangers
once, too. . . .
What makes us
Americans is our
shared commitment
to an ideal—that all of
us are created equal,
and all of us have the
chance to make of our
lives what we will.

—Address on immigration,
November 20, 2014

There must be a sustained effort to listen to each other; to learn from each other; to respect one another; and to seek common ground.

—Cairo University, June 4, 2009

For decades we've had politicians in Washington who talk about family values, but we haven't had policies that value families. . . the system is especially stacked against women, and that's why Washington has to change.

—"Change that Works for You" discussion, June 23, 2008

Hope does not arise by putting our fellow man down; it is found by lifting others up.

—Memorial for Dallas police officers, July 12, 2016

The struggle for the Voting Rights Act taught us that people who love this country can change it. Don't give away your power—go vote.

—Twitter,
August 6, 2016

I have come here to bury the last remnant of the Cold War in the Americas. I have come here to extend the hand of friendship to the Cuban people.

—Speech at the Gran Teatro, Havana, Cuba, March 22, 2016

Empowering women across the globe is not simply the right thing to do, it is also smart foreign policy.

—Presidential Proclamation, Women's History Month, February 28, 2011

We didn't raise the Statue of Liberty with her back to the world, we did it with her light shining as a beacon to the world. . . . generations of immigrants have made this country into what it is. It's what makes us special.

—Remarks on immigration, November 21, 2014

We come from different parties, but we are Americans first. And that's why disagreement cannot mean dysfunction. It can't degenerate into hatred. The American people's hopes and dreams are what matters, not ours.

—On the budget deal, October 17, 2013

Hi everybody! Back to the original handle. Is this thing still on?

—Personal Twitter, January 20, 2017

Every single one of you has something that you're good at. Every single one of you has something to offer. And you have a responsibility to yourself to discover what that is. That's the opportunity an education can provide.

—Address to America's schoolchildren, September 8, 2009

Here is something none of my predecessors ever got a chance to say: Welcome to the White House the World Series Champion, Chicago Cubs! . . . even I was not crazy enough to suggest that during these eight years we would see the Cubs win the World Series. But I did say that there's never been anything false about hope.

—Remarks honoring the World Series Champion Chicago Cubs, January 16, 2017

Never forget that honor, like character, is what you do when nobody is looking.

—Commencement address,
US Naval Academy,
May 20, 2013

MEDIA DECK

Sometimes it's not enough just to change the laws, you got to change hearts. And sports has a way, sometimes, of changing hearts in a way that politics or business doesn't.... that tells us a little something about what America is and what America can be.

—Remarks honoring the World Series Champion Chicago Cubs, January 16, 2017

In today's world, we're threatened less by evil empires and more by failing states.

—State of the Union address,
January 12, 2016

Politics has never been for the thin-skinned or the faint of heart, and if you enter the arena, you should expect to get roughed up.

—Commencement address, University of Michigan, May 1, 2010

The
character
of nations
is tested in
war, but it
is defined
in peace.

—Pearl Harbor,
December 27, 2016

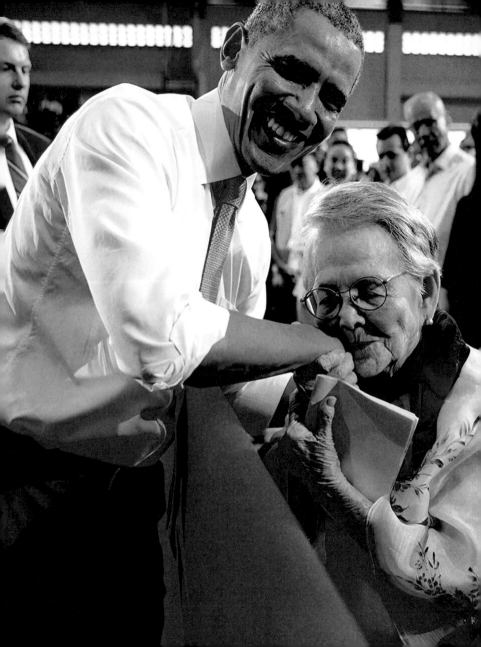

She helped me understand that America is great not because it is perfect but because it can always be made better—and that the unfinished work of perfecting our union falls to each of us.

—On his mother, "A Letter to My Daughters," *Parade*, August 4, 2013

We choose hope over fear. . . . We reject fatalism or cynicism when it comes to human affairs. We choose to work for the world as it should be, as our children deserve it to be.

—Address to the United Nations General Assembly, September 24, 2014

The thing about hip-hop today is it's smart, it's insightful. The way they can communicate a complex message in a very short space is remarkable.

—Interview with *BET*, 2008

Our television shows should have some Muslim characters that are unrelated to national security, because it's not that hard to do.

—Addressing the Islamic Society of Baltimore,
February 3, 2016

I've said and I mean it—
if anyone can put
together a plan that
is demonstrably
better than the
improvements we've
made to our health
care system and that
covers as many people
at less cost, I will
publicly support it.

—Farewell address,
January 10, 2017

In Cuba, we are ending a policy that was long past its expiration date. When what you're doing doesn't work for fifty years, it's time to try something new.

—State of the Union address, January 20, 2015

It is not
in our character
to sit idly by
as victims of fate
or circumstance,
for we are a
people of action
and innovation,
forever pushing the
boundaries of what's
possible.

—University of Iowa,
May 29, 2007

I may be a little grayer than I was eight years ago, but this is what a feminist looks like.

—United State of Women Summit,
June 14, 2016

The most challenging, most fulfilling, most important job I will have during my time on this Earth is to be Sasha and Malia's dad.

—Father's Day address, June 21, 2010

The shift to a cleaner energy economy won't happen overnight, and it will require tough choices along the way. But the debate is settled. Climate change is a fact. And when our children's children look us in the eye and ask if we did all we could to leave them a safer, more stable world, with new sources of energy, I want us to be able to say yes, we did.

—State of the Union address, January 28, 2014

Today should
also give us hope
that on the many
issues with which
we grapple, often
painfully, real
change is possible.
Shifts in hearts and
minds is possible.

—On the Supreme Court decision on marriage equality,
June 26, 2015

Don't just get involved. Fight for your seat at the table. Better yet, fight for a seat at the head of the table.

—Commencement address, Barnard College, May 14, 2012

That's our most important mission, to make sure our kids and our grandkids have at least as beautiful a planet, and hopefully more beautiful, than the one that we have. And today, I'm a little more confident that we can get the job done.

—Remarks on the Paris Agreement, October 5, 2016

Equality is not just an abstraction, it's not just a formality. It has to go hand in hand with economic opportunity.

—Congressional Black Caucus Foundation dinner, September 22, 2013

Young people have helped lead all our great movements. How inspiring to see it again in so many smart, fearless students standing up for their right to be safe; marching and organizing to remake the world as it should be. We've been waiting for you. And we've got your backs.

—Twitter,
February 22, 2018

America is a place where you can write your own destiny.

—On the Supreme Court decision
on marriage equality,
June 26, 2015

Here, we don't just commemorate victory, as proud of that victory as we are. We don't just honor sacrifice, as grateful as the world is. We come to remember why America and our allies gave so much for the survival of liberty at its moment of maximum peril. We come to tell the story of the men and women who did it so that it remains seared into the memory of a future world.

—70th Anniversary of D-Day, June 6, 2014

One of the things that makes America unique is our ability to attract talent from all around the world, to study at some of our greatest universities, and for us to have very practical, reasoned, fact-based empirical ways to figure out how we can make the world a slightly better place.

—Meeting with the 2016 American Nobel Prize winners,
November 30, 2016

There are many who won't agree with every decision or policy I make as president, and we know the government can't solve every problem. But I will always be honest with you about the challenges we face. I will listen to you, especially when we disagree.

—Victory speech, November 5, 2008

The United States of America remains the most powerful nation on Earth, and I believe that we will remain such for decades to come. But we are one nation among many.

—On the Iran nuclear deal,
August 5, 2015

We enjoy the hotdogs, we enjoy the burgers, we enjoy the barbecue. . . . But it's important to remember what a miracle this country is. How incredibly lucky we are that people, generations ago, were willing to take up arms and fight for our freedom.

—July 4, 2016

We have to
all shoulder the
responsibility
for keeping
the planet
habitable,
or we're going
to suffer the
consequences—
together.

—Georgetown University,
June 25, 2013

Expressing simple outrage without follow-up is often counter-productive.

—*GQ* Interview,
November 17, 2015

They're smart and funny, but most importantly they're kind. They don't have an attitude.

—On his daughters,
The Tonight Show,
January 18, 2009

The road we have taken to this point has not been easy. But then again, the road to change never is.

—NAACP Fight for Freedom Fund Dinner, May 1, 2005

Jimmy got his start years ago on *The Man Show*. In Washington, that's what we call a congressional hearing on contraception.

—White House Correspondents' Dinner, April 28, 2012

And this is just another example of why the holidays here at the White House are so special. Last week, I pardoned a turkey. Tonight, we're lighting the National Christmas Tree. This one is easier because a tree does not move. It does not gobble.

—Lighting of the National Christmas Tree,
December 1, 2016

Cutting the deficit by gutting our investments in innovation and education is like lightening an overloaded airplane by removing its engine. It may make you feel like you're flying high at first, but it won't take long before you feel the impact.

—State of the Union address, January 25, 2011

If you doubt America's commitment—or mine—to see that justice is done, just ask Osama bin Laden.

—State of the Union address, January 12, 2016

Just as the contributions that our servicemen and women make to this nation don't end when they take off their uniform, neither do our obligations to them.

—Arlington National Cemetery, November 11, 2009

Slamming the door in the face of refugees would betray our deepest values. That's not who we are. And it's not what we're going to do.

—Twitter, November 18, 2015

I am joined by researchers who invent some of the most advanced metals on the planet, designers who are modeling prototypes in the digital cloud, folks from the Pentagon who help to support their work. Basically, I'm here to announce that we're building Iron Man. I'm gonna blast off in a second. This has been a secret project we've been working on for a long time. Not really. Maybe. It's classified.

—On manufacturing innovation,
February 25, 2014

When we work hard, treat others with respect, spend within our means, and contribute to our communities, those are the lessons our children learn.

—"We Need Fathers to Step Up," *Parade*, June 16, 2011

Enduring security and lasting peace do not require perpetual war.

—Second Inaugural Address,
January 21, 2013

I see what's possible when we recognize that we are one American family, all deserving of equal treatment, all deserving of equal respect.

—Memorial for Dallas police officers, July 12, 2016

If we think that we can secure our country by just talking tough without acting tough and smart, then we will misunderstand this moment and miss its opportunities. If we think that we can use the same partisan playbook where we just challenge our opponent's patriotism to win an election, then the American people will lose.

—Veterans of Foreign Wars Convention, August 19, 2008

Everyone please take your seats, or else Clint Eastwood will yell at them.

—Alfred E. Smith Memorial Foundation Dinner, October 18, 2012

Successful entrepreneurs have a unique responsibility to reach back and help those hoping to follow in their footsteps.

—Facebook,
June 24, 2016

Progress does not compel us to settle centuries-long debates about the role of government for all time, but it does require us to act in our time.

—Second Inaugural Address,
January 21, 2013

If the people cannot trust their government to do the job for which it exists— to protect them and to promote their common welfare—all else is lost.

—"An Honest Government, A Hopeful Future" speech, August 28, 2006

There is a humility that comes out of this office, because you feel that no matter how much you've done, there's more work to do.

—NPR Interview, July 1, 2016

We ask for nothing more than the chance to blaze our own trail. And yet each of us is only here because somebody, somewhere, helped us find our path.

—Lake Area Technical Institute,
May 8, 2015

It's a privilege to be the parent of girls. And we want to make sure that no girl out there is denied her chance to learn— that no girl is prevented from making her unique contributions to the world. Because every girl—every girl—deserves our respect. And every girl deserves an education.

—Weekly address, March 7, 2015

But I have asserted a firm conviction— a conviction rooted in my faith in God and my faith in the American people— that working together we can move beyond some of our old racial wounds, and that in fact we have no choice if we are to continue on the path of a more perfect union.

—Campaign speech,
March 18, 2008

We can't be at war with any other religion because the world's religions are a part of the very fabric of the United States.

—Addressing the Islamic Society of Baltimore, February 3, 2016

I believe that you should look to the future with hope; not the false promise which insists that things are better than they really are, or the blind optimism that says all your problems can go away tomorrow.

—Speech at the Gran Teatro, Havana, Cuba, March 22, 2016

Every day, the White House receives thousands of letters from Americans across the country. Every night, I read 10 of them. These letters are my chance to hear directly from the people I serve—and it's one of my favorite parts of the day.

—Facebook, August 26, 2016

After a very public mix-up, my communications team has provided me with an easy way to distinguish between *Star Trek* and *Star Wars*. Spock is what Maureen Dowd calls me. Darth Vader is what John Boehner calls me.

—Gridiron Club Dinner,
March 9, 2013

In the words of one of my favorite *Star Trek* characters—Captain James T. Kirk of the USS *Enterprise*—"May the force be with you."

—Gridiron Club Dinner,
March 9, 2013

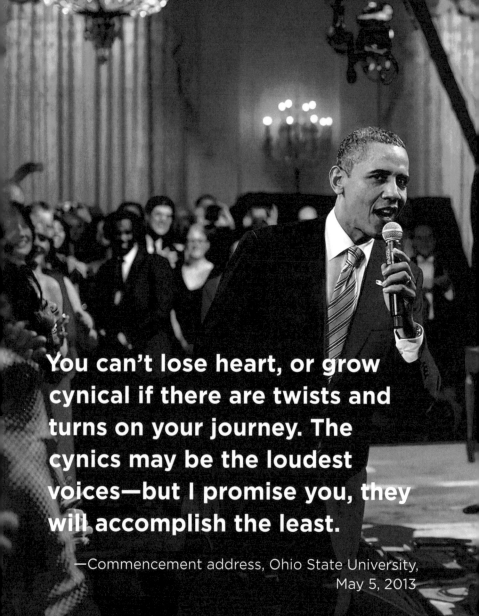

You can't lose heart, or grow cynical if there are twists and turns on your journey. The cynics may be the loudest voices—but I promise you, they will accomplish the least.

—Commencement address, Ohio State University, May 5, 2013

Thomas Jefferson's opponents tried to stir things up by suggesting he was a Muslim— so I was not the first. It's true. Look it up.

—Addressing the Islamic Society of Baltimore, February 3, 2016

We did not come to fear the future; we came here to shape it.

—Speech to Congress on health care reform, September 9, 2009

Partnership among nations is not a choice; it is the one way, the only way, to protect our common security and advance our common humanity.

—Campaign speech,
July 24, 2008

If you've been successful, you didn't get there on your own. I'm always struck by people who think, "Well, it must be because I was just so smart." There are a lot of smart people out there. "It must be because I worked harder than everybody else." Let me tell you something: there are a whole bunch of hardworking people out there.

—Campaign event,
July 13, 2012

It's important for us to pause for a moment and make sure that we're talking with each other in a way that heals, not in a way that wounds.

—Memorial for victims of Tucson shooting, January 12, 2011

Dr. King was 26 when the Montgomery bus boycott began. He started small, rallying others who believed their efforts mattered, pressing on through challenges and doubts to change our world for the better. A permanent inspiration for the rest of us to keep pushing towards justice.

—Twitter, January 15, 2018

The strongest foundation for human progress lies in open economies, open societies, and open governments. To put it simply, democracy, more than any other form of government, delivers for our citizens. And I believe that truth will only grow stronger in a world where the borders between nations are blurred.

—Address to the United Nations General Assembly, September 23, 2010

Making your mark on the world is hard. If it were easy, everybody would do it.

—Campus Progress
Annual Conference,
July 12, 2006

If you were successful, somebody along the line gave you some help. There was a great teacher somewhere in your life. Somebody helped to create this unbelievable American system that we have that allowed you to thrive. Somebody invested in roads and bridges. If you've got a business, you didn't build that. Somebody else made that happen.

—Campaign event,
July 13, 2012

You've got these $10,000-a-plate dinners, Golden Circle Clubs. I think when the average voter looks at that, they rightly feel they've been locked out of the process.

—*The Audacity of Hope,*
2006

The way things are set up right now isn't always fair for people, and that motivates you, because you say, well, I can't make everything perfect, I can't prevent somebody from getting sick, but maybe I can make sure that they've got insurance so that when they do get sick, they're going to get some help.

—Wakefield High School,
September 8, 2009

I am president, I am not king. I can't do these things just by myself.

—Interview, *Univision*, October 25, 2010

We only
get one
home.
We only
get one
planet.
There's
no plan B.

—Announcing the
Clean Power Plan,
August 3, 2015

Six years into my presidency some people still say I'm arrogant, aloof, condescending. Some people are so dumb.

—White House
Correspondents' Dinner,
April 25, 2015

To my 5th grade teacher Ms. Mabel Hefty and the educators who inspire our young people every single day: Thank you.

—Twitter, May 3, 2016

I'm the attorney general's boss. If I chime in with a strong opinion about what's happened, not only do I stand to potentially damage subsequent law-enforcement cases, but immediately you get blowback and backlash that may make people less open to listening.

—*GQ* Interview, November 17, 2015

You didn't elect me to tell you what you wanted to hear. You elected me to tell you the truth.

—Democratic National Convention,
September 6, 2012

I've always drawn inspiration from what Dr. King called life's most persistent and urgent question: "What are you doing for others?"

—Twitter, January 21, 2019

All of us have to recognize that being a man is first and foremost being a good human. That means being responsible, being reliable, working hard, being kind, being respectful, being compassionate. . .

. . .If you're confident about your strength, you don't need to show me by putting somebody else down. Show me how strong you are by lifting somebody else up.

—Interview with Steph Curry,
My Brother's Keeper event,
February 19, 2019

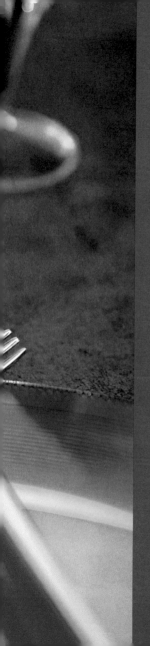

All they have to offer is the same prescriptions they've had for the last 30 years. Have a surplus? Try a tax cut. Deficit too high? Try another. Feel a cold coming on? Take two tax cuts, roll back some regulations, and call us in the morning.

—Democratic National Convention, September 6, 2012

We're part of a long-running story. We just try to get our paragraph right.

—"Going the Distance," *The New Yorker*, January 27, 2014

Where you start should not determine where you end up.

—College Opportunity Summit,
December 4, 2014

If anybody still wants to dispute the science around climate change, have at it. You will be pretty lonely, because you'll be debating our military, most of America's business leaders, the majority of the American people, almost the entire scientific community, and two hundred nations around the world who agree it's a problem and intend to solve it.

—State of the Union address,
January 12, 2016

A decade after 9/11, it's clear for all the world to see—the terrorists who attacked us that September morning are no match for the character of our people, the resilience of our nation, or the endurance of our values.

—September 10, 2011

The battle lines may have shifted and the barriers to equality may be new, but what's not new is the need for everyday heroes to stand up and speak out for what they believe is right.

—NAACP Fight for Freedom Fund Dinner,
May 1, 2005

I think about all
the struggles that
a lot of people
are going through
around the country
and I say to myself,
it's such an honor
to be in this job;
I can't afford to
get tired.

—Wakefield High School,
September 8, 2009

In politics and in life, ignorance is not a virtue. It's not cool to not know what you're talking about. That's not keeping it real, or telling it like it is. That's not challenging political correctness. That's just not knowing what you're talking about.

—Commencement address, Rutgers University, May 15, 2016

Launching a pilot program to help students in prison pay for college, because everyone willing to work for it deserves a second chance.

—Twitter, July 31, 2015

Politics depends on our ability to persuade each other of common aims based on a common reality. It involves the compromise, the art of what's possible.

—Keynote speech,
Building a Covenant for a New America Conference,
June 28, 2006

The future rewards those who press on.

—Congressional Black Caucus Foundation dinner, September 24, 2011

We're not a fragile people. We're not a frightful people. Our power doesn't come from some self-declared savior promising that he alone can restore order as long as we do things his way. We don't look to be ruled.

—Democratic National Convention, July 27, 2016

We don't have time for a meeting of the Flat Earth Society.

—Georgetown University,
June 25, 2013

As nations, and as people, we cannot choose the history that we inherit. But we can choose what lessons to draw from it, and use those lessons to chart our own futures.

—Pearl Harbor,
December 27, 2016

Democracy grinds to a halt without a willingness to compromise, or when even basic facts are contested, or when we listen only to those who agree with us.

—State of the Union address,
January 12, 2016

Resist the conventional wisdom and the drumbeat of war. Worry less about being labeled weak; worry more about getting it right.

—American University,
August 5, 2015

The tired feet of those who walked the dusty roads of Montgomery helped a nation see that to which it had once been blind. It is because of these men and women that I stand here today. It is because of them that our children grow up in a land more free and more fair; a land truer to its founding creed.

—Dedication of statue honoring Rosa Parks, February 27, 2013

I think the biggest mistake politicians make is being inauthentic. By writing about my mistakes, I was trying to show how I was vulnerable to the same pitfalls as American youth everywhere.

—Interview, *O, the Oprah Magazine*, November 2004

One voice can change a room. And if the voice can change a room, it can change a city. And if it can change a city, it can change a state. And if it can change a state, it can change a nation. And if it can change a nation, it can change the world.

—Rally for health care reform, September 12, 2009

Live with integrity, and speak with honesty, and take responsibility, and demand accountability.

—Commencement address,
US Naval Academy,
May 20, 2013

No matter who you are or what you look like, if you abide by the law you should be protected by it; if you adhere to our common values you should be treated no different than anyone else.

—State of the Union address,
January 27, 2010

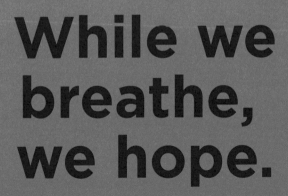

While we breathe, we hope.

—Victory speech,
November 5, 2008

A freedom which asks only "what's in it for me," a freedom without commitment to others, a freedom without love or charity or duty or patriotism is unworthy of our founding ideals and those who died in their defense.

—Democratic National Convention, September 6, 2012

If this material works well, I'm going to use it at Goldman Sachs next year. Earn me some serious Tubmans.

—White House Correspondents' Dinner, April 30, 2016

You want everybody to act like adults, quit playing games, realize it's not just "My way or the highway."

—Remarks to the press, April 6, 2011

We need leaders in Congress who know the American Dream is not something that a wall can contain.

—Hillary Clinton campaign rally,
September 13, 2016

It's hard to preach to an empty stomach. If people have severe, immediate material needs—shelter, food, clothing—then that is their focus. Economic growth and development that is self-sustaining can liberate people.

—Town hall with students, Mumbai, India, November 7, 2010

Freedom is not an abstract idea; freedom is the very thing that makes human progress possible— not just at the ballot box, but in our daily lives.

—University of Yangon, Rangoon, Burma, November 19, 2012

This decision affirms what millions of Americans already believe in their hearts: When all Americans are treated as equal we are all more free.

—On the Supreme Court decision on marriage equality, June 26, 2015

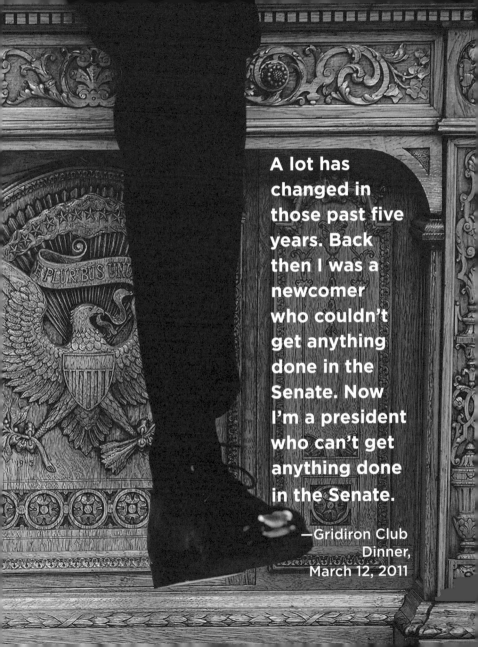

A lot has changed in those past five years. Back then I was a newcomer who couldn't get anything done in the Senate. Now I'm a president who can't get anything done in the Senate.

—Gridiron Club Dinner, March 12, 2011

We must change our mindset about war itself—to prevent conflict through diplomacy, and strive to end conflicts after they've begun... Above all, we must reimagine our connection to one another as members of one human race.

—Hiroshima Peace Memorial, May 27, 2016

I never suggested that change would be easy, or that I could do it alone. Democracy in a nation of 300 million people can be noisy and messy and complicated. And when you try to do big things and make big changes, it stirs passions and controversy. That's just how it is.

—State of the Union address,
January 27, 2010

It shows a poverty of ambition to just want to take more and more and more, instead of saying, "Wow, I've got so much. Who can I help?"

—Honoring Nelson Mandela, July 17, 2018

My parents shared not only an improbable love; they shared an abiding faith in the possibilities of this nation. They would give me an African name, Barack, or "blessed," believing that in a tolerant America your name is no barrier to success.

They imagined me going to the best schools in the land, even though they weren't rich, because in a generous America you don't have to be rich to achieve your potential.

—Keynote address, Democratic National Convention, July 27, 2004

What we can do, as flawed as we are, is still see God in other people and do our best to help them find their own grace.

—Town hall,
September 28, 2010

Dropping bombs on someone to prove that you're willing to drop bombs on someone is just about the worst reason to use force.

—*The Atlantic,*
April 2016

We gather because we have chosen hope over fear, unity of purpose over conflict and discord.

—Inaugural address, January 20, 2009

The ultimate success of democracy in the world won't come because the United States dictates it; it will come because individual citizens demand a say in how they are governed.

—Address to the
United Nations
General Assembly,
September 23, 2010

For all the cruelty and hardship of our world, we are not mere prisoners of fate. Our actions matter, and can bend history in the direction of justice.

—Nobel Prize Acceptance speech, December 10, 2009

In the end, it's our ideals, our values that built America—values that allowed us to forge a nation made up of immigrants from every corner of the globe; values that drive our citizens still.

—State of the Union address, January 27, 2010

If you swiped through my music collection, you'd find some Bruce, some Stevie, some Al Green. If you opened my iPad, you'd find the word puzzle games I love to play. If you looked at my bookshelf, you'd find Marilynne Robinson novels and Toni Morrison classics.

—Facebook,
April 28, 2016

What Washington needs is adult supervision.

—Fundraising letter,
October 2006

Have principles and issues you are passionate about, and act; worry more about doing something than being something.

—Advice for an aspiring politician,
Twitter, July 1, 2015

The arc of the moral universe may bend towards justice, but it doesn't bend on its own.

—50th anniversary of the March on Washington, Lincoln Memorial, August 28, 2013

The time has come for a president who will be honest about the choices and the challenges we face; who will listen to you and learn from you even when we disagree; who won't just tell you what you want to hear, but what you need to know.

—Iowa caucus, January 3, 2008

Today is a big step in our march toward equality. Gay and lesbian couples now have the right to marry, just like anyone else. #LoveWins.

—Twitter, June 26, 2015

Climate change is a fact. And when our children's children look us in the eye and ask if we did all we could to leave them a safer, more stable world, with new sources of energy, I want us to be able to say yes, we did.

—State of the Union address, January 28, 2014

As we get older, we learn we don't always have control of things—not even a President does. But we do have control over how we respond to the world. We do have control over how we treat one another.

—Memorial for Dallas police officers, July 12, 2016

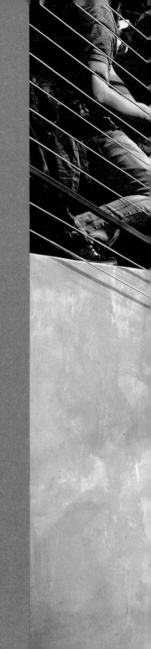

We may not be able to stop all evil in the world, but I know that how we treat one another, that's entirely up to us.

—Memorial for victims of Tucson shooting, January 12, 2011

We have to start with the premise that each of our fellow citizens loves this country just as much as we do; that they value hard work and family just like we do; that their children are just as curious and hopeful and worthy of love as our own.

—Farewell address, January 10, 2017

If those Republicans come at me with the same fear-mongering and swift-boating that they usually do, then I will take them head on. Because I believe the American people are tired of fear and tired of distractions and tired of diversions.

We can make this election not about fear, but about the future. And that won't just be a Democratic victory; that will be an American victory.

—Jefferson-Jackson Dinner,
November 10, 2007

You can't let your failures define you—you have to let your failures teach you.

—Wakefeld High School,
September 8, 2009

I suspect that those of you who pursue more education, or climb the corporate ladder, or enter the arts or science or journalism, you will still choose a cause that you care about in your life and will fight like heck to realize your vision. There is a word for this. It's citizenship.

—Commencement address, Ohio State University, May 5, 2013

Some folks still don't think I spend enough time with Congress. "Why don't you get a drink with Mitch McConnell?" they ask. Really? Why don't *you* get a drink with Mitch McConnell?

—White House Correspondents' Dinner, April 27, 2013

Nothing can stand in the way of the power of millions of voices calling for change.

—Primary speech,
January 8, 2008

You can't separate good policy from the need to bring the American people along and make sure that they know why you're doing what you're doing.

—*GQ* Interview, November 17, 2015

You were
the change. You
answered people's
hopes, and because
of you, by almost
every measure,
America is a better,
stronger place
than it was
when we started.

—Farewell address,
January 10, 2017

Sometimes there are days like this, when that slow, steady effort is rewarded with justice that arrives like a thunderbolt.

—On the Supreme Court decision on marriage equality, June 26, 2015

Hope is that thing inside us that insists, despite all the evidence to the contrary, that something better awaits us if we have the courage to reach for it, and to work for it, and to fight for it.

—Campaign speech, January 3, 2008

In a world of complex threats, our security and leadership depends on all elements of our power— including strong and principled diplomacy.

—State of the Union address, January 28, 2014

This generation of climate activists is tired of inaction, and they've caught the attention of leaders all over the world. So while this challenge is only getting more urgent, they show us the kind of action it'll take to meet this moment.

—Twitter, April 22, 2019

Democracy isn't a spectator sport.

—Democratic National Convention,
July 27, 2016

Change is the effort of committed citizens who hitch their wagons to something bigger than themselves and fight for it every single day.

—Commencement address, Howard University, May 7, 2016

Don't boo. Vote.

—Democratic National Convention,
July 27, 2016

Whether we've seen eye-to-eye or rarely agreed at all, my conversations with you, the American people—in living rooms and schools; at farms and on factory floors; at diners and on distant military outposts—are what have kept me honest, kept me inspired, and kept me going. Every day, I learned from you. You made me a better President, and you made me a better man.

—Final Weekly Address, January 14, 2017

We are
the ones
we've been
waiting for.
We are the
change that
we seek.

—Campaign speech,
February 5, 2008

When I no longer hold this office, I will be right there with you as a citizen, inspired by those voices of fairness and vision, of grit and good humor and kindness that helped America travel so far.

—State of the Union address, January 12, 2016

Eight years ago, I said it was time to change the tone of our politics. In hindsight, I clearly should have been more specific.

—White House Correspondents' Dinner, April 30, 2016

Gays and lesbians and transgender persons are our brothers, our sisters, our children, our cousins, our friends, our co-workers. . . they've got to be treated like every other American.

—Press conference,
June 29, 2011

The Constitution prohibits it, but, more importantly, Michelle prohibits it.

—On serving one more term, June 1, 2016

The world is more interconnected than ever before, and it's becoming more connected every day. Building walls won't change that.

—Commencement address, Rutgers University, May 15, 2016

I'm not going to talk long because I want to shake as many hands as possible—although I still got to apply the "no selfie rule" because otherwise I'm here for like four hours.

—Congressional Picnic,
June 15, 2016

But our country is not just all about the Benjamins—it's about the Tubmans, too. We need all our young people to know that Clara Barton and Lucretia Mott and Sojourner Truth and Eleanor Roosevelt and Dorothy Height, those aren't just for Women's History Month.

They're the authors of our history, women who shaped their destiny. They need to know that.

—United State of Women Summit,
June 14, 2016

I think you, like I, believe that politics can be a noble endeavor, and that a politics that better reflects our people is not only possible, but it couldn't be more important.

—2016 National Governors Association Dinner, February 21, 2016

But some of the best moments that I've had as President have involved science and our annual Science Fair. I mean, I have shot a marshmallow out of a cannon directly under Lincoln's portrait.

—White House Science Fair,
April 13, 2016

As Commander-in-Chief, I have no more solemn obligation than leading our men and women in uniform. Making sure they have what they need to succeed. Making sure we only send them into harm's way when it's absolutely necessary.

—Weekly Address,
Remembering Our Fallen Heroes,
May 28, 2016

America is a nation that is a constant work in progress. That's why we are exceptional. We don't stop.

—Black History Month Reception, February 18, 2016

Each of us as leaders, each nation can choose to reject those who appeal to our worst impulses and embrace those who appeal to our best. For we have shown that we can choose a better history.

—Address to the United Nations General Assembly, September 20, 2016

The office [of the Presidency] humbles you. You're reminded daily that in this great democracy, you are but a relay swimmer in the currents of history, bound by decisions made by those who came before, reliant on the efforts of those who will follow to fully vindicate your vision.

—Lyndon B. Johnson Presidential Library Civil Rights Summit, Austin, Texas, April 10, 2014

People always ask me about Roswell and the aliens and UFOs, and it turns out the stuff going on that's top secret isn't nearly as exciting as you expect.

—*GQ* Interview, November 17, 2015

You have to go through life with more than just passion for change; you need a strategy. I'll repeat that. I want you to have passion, but you have to have a strategy. Not just awareness, but action. Not just hashtags, but votes.

—Commencement address, Howard University, May 7, 2016

There are those who will continue to tell us we cannot do this. That we cannot have what we long for. That we are peddling false hopes.

But here's what I know. I know that when people say we can't overcome all the big money and influence in Washington, I think of the elderly woman who sent me a contribution the other day—an envelope that had a money order for $3.01 along with a verse of scripture tucked inside. So don't tell us change isn't possible.

—South Carolina Primary Victory speech, January 26, 2008

Image Credits